YORK NOTES

KS2 ENGLISH SATS

CATCH UP READING

WENDY CHERRY AND EMMA WILKINSON

Pearson

YORK PRESS

YORK PRESS
322 Old Brompton Road, London SW5 9JH

PEARSON EDUCATION LIMITED
Edinburgh Gate, Harlow,
Essex CM20 2JE, United Kingdom
Associated companies, branches and representatives throughout the world

First published 2018

10 9 8 7 6 5 4 3 2 1

ISBN 978–1–2922–3283–6

Typeset by Kamae Design
Printed in Slovakia

Image credits:

CONTENTS

Check Out Summarising!

Check Out Inferences!

Check Out Making Predictions!

Check Out Making Comparisons!

Answers and Glossary

GET TO KNOW SATS QUESTIONS!
MULTIPLE CHOICE

In this section, we'll explain the types of questions you will have to answer in the SATs tests.

1 **Multiple choice questions have answers for you to choose from. You must read the question carefully and choose the correct answer from the options.**

Paul was exhausted. He couldn't walk any further.

Q: Which word best describes how Paul felt? Tick **one**.

happy ☐

excited ☐

tired ☑

angry ☐

Good answer: *tired*

2 **How do you choose the correct answer?**

- **Cover the answers** before you read the question.

- **Ask yourself**: *Do you already know the answer?*

- **Look at the options** and **choose the one that is closest to your answer.**

- If you don't know the answer, **cross out** the options that you know are wrong, then **re-read the text for clues** and choose from the remaining answers.

TOP TIP ⭐

If you still don't know the answer, **have a guess**! You've got nothing to lose!

NOW YOU TRY!

Lucy was shivering and her heart was thumping.

This tells us that Lucy was ...

Tick **one**.

... hot and excited. ☐

... cold and scared. ☑

... cold and relaxed. ☐

... hot and anxious. ☐

RANKING/ORDERING

 Sometimes you will be asked to order events to show when they happen **in the text.**

Q: Number the following events 1–5 to show the order in which they happen in the story of Little Red Riding Hood. The first one has been done for you.

A Little Red Riding Hood sets off with some food.

B The wolf finds out where Granny lives.

C The wolf goes to Granny's house.

D Little Red Riding Hood's mother asks her to visit her Granny.

E Little Red Riding Hood meets a wolf.

Good answer: *A 2; B 4; C 5; D 1; E 3*

② **How do you order information?**

- **Read all the options first.** You may be able to work out the first and last event, but it is harder to order the events in the middle.

- **Look back at the text** to help you.

- **Always check the order.** Read each sentence in the order you've numbered them and check the sequence. Does the order match the text? Is anything in the wrong place?

TOP TIP ⭐

Think about the main things that happen and make a list in your head. Try <u>underlining</u> the events in the text to show the order more clearly.

NOW YOU TRY!

Number the sentences 1–5 to show the order for writing a letter.

Put a stamp on the envelope. 5

Get a piece of paper and an envelope. 1

Seal the envelope. 4

Write your letter. 2

Put the letter in the envelope. 3

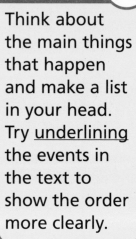

MATCHING AND LABELLING

1 **Matching and labelling** show that you understand what you are reading. **You should be able to make links between** key words **and the** main content.

Q: Draw lines to match each section to the correct content. One has been done for you.

Section

1 The first explorers

2 Frequently asked questions

3 Safety problems

4 A personal achievement

Content

A information about the dangers of exploration

B information about an individual

C questions and answers about exploration

D information about early explorers

Good answer: *1 D; 2 C; 3 A; 4 B*

2 **How do we** match information?

- **Read the instructions carefully.** Make sure you know what you have to do. You might be asked to draw lines, tick a box or choose a heading.

- **Look for key words and clues.** In the example, we can match number **3** to part **A** because the words *safety problems* and *danger* give us clues that these parts are related.

- **Look back at the text** to check what it actually says.

- **Read to understand the general meaning.** You do not need to understand every word.

TOP TIP ★

Sometimes you will be asked to choose a title for a text. This is another type of matching task, but you can follow the same steps.

NOW YOU TRY!

It was a wonderful achievement. Laura won five medals for her country, but she had worked very hard to achieve this great result.

Choose the best title for the text. Tick **one**.

A lucky win ☐   Winning easily ☐

A hard-earned win ☐   An easy achievement ☐

FIND AND COPY

❶ You may be asked to find a word (or words) in a text. This is to show that you understand the meaning.

> *The old cat staggered into view. It was tired and hungry and limped along the road.*

Q: **Find** and **copy two** words that tell us how the cat walked.

Good answer: 1. *staggered*   2. *limped*

❷ How do you find the right words?

- **Think** about the **type of words** you need to find. In the example you are looking for two words that tell us about the way the cat moved (verbs).

- **Underline possible words** in the text.

- **Read the text closely** and try to work out the meaning of each word.

❸ You may be asked to find and copy a group of words.

> *Luke shook with fear when he saw the scary monster. It was walking slowly towards him.*

Q: **Find** and **copy** a group of words that tell you Luke was scared.

Good answer: *Luke shook with fear.*

TOP TIP ⭐

Be careful! Don't get distracted by words that sound similar. We know the monster is *scary*, but this doesn't tell us that Luke was actually *scared*.

NOW YOU TRY!

> *Ben looked at the empty beach. The waves were thundering on the sand as the rain started to fall.*

a) **Find** and **copy one** word that tells us that no one else was around.

....

b) **Find** and **copy** a group of words that tell us the weather was bad.

....

SHORT RESPONSE AND OPEN-ENDED RESPONSE

① **Different questions need different types of answers. Some answers only need one or two words, but others need a sentence or two. Sometimes a longer answer is needed.**

Ruth walked into the room. Alice smiled when she saw her.

Q: How do you think Alice felt when Ruth arrived?

Good answer: *She was happy.*

② **How do you know what type of answer to give?**

- The length and number of answer lines gives you a clue. A **short answer line** shows that only **one or two words** are needed.

- **One or two longer lines** shows that a **sentence** is needed.

- **More than two writing lines** shows that a **more detailed answer** is needed.

- Sometimes you will just need to **tick a box or draw a line** to the correct answer.

- If a question is worth **two marks**, sometimes you'll get **one mark for giving an answer and one for using evidence from the text.**

- You may be asked to give **two or more** pieces of information.

TOP TIP ⭐

You might be asked to use information from the text to back up your answer. If in doubt, give a reason for your answer using '... **because the text says** ...'.

TOP TIP ⭐

The number of marks shows how many parts there should be to your answer!

NOW YOU TRY!

Thomas saw the spiders. He screamed and ran as fast as he could.

Why did Thomas run away? How do you know this?

....

....

....

.... (2 marks)

9

In this section we'll look at the important reading skills that will help you tackle the questions in the SATs tests.

1 **It is important to** read the questions carefully **so that you give the correct information.**

Sanjay packed his suitcase. He had so much to take that he had to sit on the case to zip it up. He would miss his brother, Raj, but it would be a great adventure.

Q: **Who** is going away?

Good answer: *Sanjay*

Q: **Why** did he sit on the suitcase?

Good answer: *The suitcase was too full and wouldn't shut.*

2 **How do you answer the questions** accurately?

- **Read the question slowly and underline any key words.** Do you understand what you are being asked?

- Is the question asking **Who, Why, What** or **How**? This will give you a clue about the answer. E.g. **Who** tells you the answer will be a character or a person. **Why** and sometimes **How** tells you that you need to give a reason.

- Do you need to find specific **word classes**, e.g. a **noun, verb** or **adjective**, or do you need to give an **explanation**?

NOW YOU TRY!

The forest was gloomy and damp. The trees stood spookily like long-fingered hands waiting to grab him. All at once there was a deafening noise ...

a) Write **one** word that tells you that it was dark in the forest.

....

b) How do you know that the character might be scared?

....

....

TOP TIP

Check whether you need to give **one** or **two** pieces of information and that you have answered the question.

HINT!

You are looking for an **adjective**. Which word that describes the forest can be replaced with the adjective *dark*?

HINT!

The question asks *How....* Make sure you explain your answer.

1 **Sometimes you have to skim a text to find the main information or get the main idea without reading all of it. This is useful if you have a long text and need to answer general questions about it.**

A very different school trip

Sam's day trip started early in the morning, before the sun came up. All twenty of the children had their bags, jackets, hats and coats. Sam and some of his younger friends were nervous.

However, by the end of Sunday he felt very different. They'd been on an adventure to an exciting new theme park and he was very happy!

Q: What is the text about?

Good answer: *The text is about a trip.*

HINT!

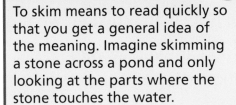

To skim means to read quickly so that you get a general idea of the meaning. Imagine skimming a stone across a pond and only looking at the parts where the stone touches the water.

2 **How do you skim a text?**

- **Skimming a text** helps you to decide if you need to read it in more detail. If none of the information you skim read is relevant, then you can keep going until you **find a part that might contain the answer.**

- **Read the title,** if there is one, to get a clue about the content.

- **Read the first sentence** in each **paragraph.**

- You can also **read a few words** within each paragraph so that you understand the main idea of each part, but you **do not need to read every word.**

NOW YOU TRY!

Which paragraph in the example text *A very different school trip* tells you what Sam thought about the trip at the end of the day?

....

TOP TIP

Skimming a text is a useful skill to help you answer lots of different question types. Once you find the right place in the text, you may need to read it in more detail to answer the question.

SKIM AND SCAN 2

① You can scan a text to find specific information, such as names, numbers or days. **This is useful if you have a long text and need to find** a certain word or detail **to answer a question.**

Read the example text on page 11 again.

Q: How many children went on the trip?

Good answer: *Twenty*

Read the example text on page 11 again.

Read the example text on page 11 again.

HINT!

To scan means to read quickly to find important information. Imagine a scanner in a hospital. This is used to look at (scan) the whole body to find a specific area. Only once this area is found will it be looked at in detail.

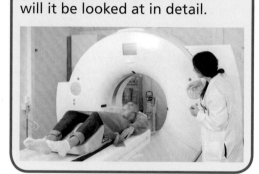

② How do you scan a text?

- **Look for key words in the questions,** and search the text for these words or synonyms of these words.

- **Run your finger along each line** until you find a relevant word. It might help to underline it.

- **Read the question carefully.** The example question uses *How many*, so you know you need to look for a number. You might need to look for days of the week, adjectives, names or dates.

- **Look for information in lists or bullet points** – these might also give key information.

TOP TIP

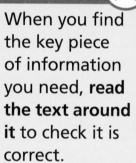

When you find the key piece of information you need, **read the text around it** to check it is correct.

HINT!

You can **skim** a longer text to find the correct place, then **scan** that section for the information you need.

NOW YOU TRY!

Read the example text on page 11 again.

What day was the trip? ....

PRACTISE AGAIN!

Answer the following questions about the example text on page 11.

a) What did the children take on the trip?

....

b) Where did the children go on the trip?

....

1 You might be asked to find information, for example to pick out relevant facts in a text. You might also need to find information to support an answer.

The house was very old. The windows were broken and dirty, and the door was crooked. Evie felt curious when she looked at the house. It looked like nobody had lived there for a very long time. The garden at the front was full of weeds. A grey cat was sitting on the wall next to a large tree, and it hissed at Evie angrily, as if she shouldn't be there.

Q: What are we told about the garden?

Good Answer: *It was full of weeds.*

2 How do you find information?

- **Read the question carefully** to see what information you need to find. In the example, you need to look for the word *garden*.

- **Scan** the text for the word *garden*.

- **Look at the text around the important word(s)** to find the information you need to answer the question.

TOP TIP

You can **underline or highlight** words in the text that might help you answer the question. This will help you to find them again quickly if you need to.

NOW YOU TRY!

Read the example text above again.

How did Evie feel when she looked at the house?

....

You may have to find more than one piece of information in a text in order to explain or describe something in detail. It can be useful to make notes.

Read the example text on page 13 again.

Q: What words does the writer use to describe the house and the windows?

Good answer: *The house was old. The windows were broken and dirty.*

> *Notes:*
>
> *house = old*
>
> *windows = broken, dirty*

2 How do you find information to answer more detailed questions?

- **Pick out the important information in the question.** In the example, it is likely to be **adjectives** linked to *house* and *windows* because we're asked for describing words.

- **Scan** the text for the words *house* and *windows*.

- **Write down or underline** any important words or information in the text.

- **Write your answer** in a **full sentence** using the information you have found.

NOW YOU TRY!

Read the example text on page 13 again. Find the information you need to answer the question.

Where was the cat sitting?

....

HINT!

Remember to re-read the question for clues about the information you need to find.

PRACTISE AGAIN!

Answer the following questions about the example text on page 13.

a) What does the writer say about the door?

....

b) What word shows that the cat didn't want to see Evie?

....

USE INFORMATION

❶ It is important to know **what information is useful**, as this will help you to answer the questions properly.

Alex hated getting on the bus in the mornings. The walk to the bus stop was very long, and when he got on the bus, it was always busy. He often had to stand up, and this made him feel sick. He couldn't sit down and look at a book or play a game on his phone.

Q: The text says **He often had to stand up**. How does this make Alex feel?

Good answer: *It makes him feel sick.*

❷ How do you know which **information** is useful?

- When you are given an **extract in *italics*** in the question, this tells you that it is taken directly from the text. First, **look back at the text and find the extract.** Then **read the whole sentence** or **paragraph** around the words.

- You may also be asked to find a paragraph or line which includes a particular **phrase**. This will save you re-reading the whole text and means that you can use **skimming and scanning** to locate the correct place.

- You might see a question or a section that gives you a **page number**. This is important to note as it makes sure that you are referring to the correct text.

TOP TIP ★

Read all of the information you are given in the question. This will save you a lot of time searching around for the correct place in the text.

NOW YOU TRY!

Marie put the child down like a china doll. Then she went to get her a glass of water and a warm blanket.

What does the phrase *like a china doll* in line 1 suggest about the child?

....

....

....

EXPLAIN IDEAS

① **Unless the question asks you to copy something from the text, you will need to explain ideas in your own words and might have to summarise parts of a text.**

Read this sentence from the example text on page 15:

> *He couldn't sit down and look at a book or play a game on his phone.*

Q: What does this tell us about what Alex enjoys doing on the bus?

Good answer: *Alex enjoys reading and playing on his phone.*

② **How do you explain ideas?**

- **Find the right place** in the text.

- Ask yourself **what the author is trying to tell you.**

- **Create a sentence that summarises** what is being said. Don't <u>copy</u> straight from the text unless you are asked to.

- **Check that your answer is clear and accurate.** Does it answer the question?

- The words *He couldn't* suggest that Alex is being stopped from doing something he wants to do. If he could, he would read or play on his phone = he enjoys doing these things.

TOP TIP

The ideas in the text may not be clearly stated and may be **hidden in the words**. This means you will have to **make inferences**. You will learn more about this later in the book.

NOW YOU TRY!

> *Maryam was jumping up and down. She couldn't wait another minute. It was her birthday, and she was hoping to get a new bike. She thought about the one she had seen in the shop. It was light green, with white tyres and silver handlebars.*

Why was Maryam jumping up and down?

....

HINT!

We know that it is her birthday but this doesn't explain why she is jumping up and down. Think about how she might be feeling. How would you be feeling?

Remember to explain your answer in your own words!

CHECK OUT WORD MEANINGS!
EXPLAIN WHAT WORDS MEAN 1

❶ You need to explain what words mean to show you understand what you have read.

Here, and in the rest of the book, we'll show you how to find the best answer for each type of question!

The powerful rain hammered down on the roof.

Q: What does the word **hammered** tell you about the rain?

Good answer: *It was raining very hard.*

❷ How do you work out word meanings?

- **Find the word** in the text, e.g. *hammered*.

- **Read ALL the information** around the word.
  For example: The rain is *powerful*. This means 'strong'.

- **Check** the **word class**. What type of word is it?
  Here *hammered* is a **verb**: it tells us what the rain is doing.

- **Think** of **synonyms** or related words: *hammered* is like 'hammer'.

  Ask yourself: What do you use a hammer for?

  Answer: To hit things hard!

TOP TIP ⭐

A **synonym** is a word that is **close in meaning** to another one. For example, 'hit', 'struck hard', 'clouted', 'banged' are all synonyms for 'hammered'.

NOW YOU TRY!

There were no cars and no people on the streets. The whole town was utterly deserted. All Alfie could hear was the wind whistling through the ruins.

Remember: Find, Read, Check, Think!

What does the word **deserted** tell you about the town?

It is ....

EXPLAIN WHAT WORDS MEAN 2

❶ You may need to choose an answer that has the closest meaning **to a word you have read.**

There were four of them in the group, but Lee was always getting into trouble. The others felt it was time for him to start acting his age – he was so immature.

Q: Which of the following four words is closest in meaning to *immature*? Tick **one**.

wild ☐   babyish ☐

foolish ☐   reckless ☐

Correct answer: *babyish*

❷ How do you work out the closest word meaning?

- Use the '**Find, Read, Check, Think**' tool THEN check the word itself and look for clues.

- Look at the **prefix 'im'**. This can mean '**opposite to**' or '**not**' (like '**possible**' and '**im**possible'). So, **im**mature = not mature.

- Mature = grown up, adult. So, immature = not grown up, not adult, so 'like a baby'.

TOP TIP ★

You may be given a **compound word**, such as 'password'. To work out the meaning, **break down the word!** 'Pass' = 'go through' and 'word' = 'series of letters'. So 'password' = the letters/ word that lets you through!

PRACTISE AGAIN!

Read the text.

When your computer gets very slow, you sometimes need to upgrade it and get a more powerful one. However, make sure you work out what the problem is first.

Which of these words is closest in meaning to *upgrade*?

Tick **one**.

exchange ☐   improve ☐

destroy ☐   restart ☐

1 Read the text.

The boat sailed slowly into the harbour. It was a sunny day, and the light was dazzling on the water, making it hard to see. The captain was being cautious because of the rocks. It had been a complicated journey, with lots of problems. Everyone began cheering as they arrived home.

a) What does the word **cautious** mean? Tick the correct answer.

Cautious means:

surprised ☐   excited ☐

careful ☐   thoughtless ☐

b) Which word is closest in meaning to **complicated**?

Tick one.

hard ☐

exciting ☐

easy ☐

short ☐

c) What does the word **dazzling** tell you about the light? Complete the sentence below with one of the words in the box.

quick   bright   happy   lucky

The light was very ....

Wow, you're making great progress!

→ EXPLAIN WHAT WORDS MEAN →

EXPLAIN PHRASE MEANINGS 1

❶ You might be asked to explain the meaning of a group of words. **The meaning of individual words may change when words are put together.**

Toby stood up straight away and ran to the door.

Q: What do the words **straight away** tell us about how Toby stood up?

Good answer: *He stood up quickly.*

❷ How do you work out the meaning of a phrase**?**

- **Find the phrase in the text,** e.g. *straight away.*

- **Read the phrase and the information around it.** Do the words give you clues?

  He stood up + to the door tells us Toby got up and went to the door. Then *straight away + ran* tells us he did it **quickly**.

- **Check your answer.** Ask yourself: Does your explanation make sense within the text?

  *Toby stood up **quickly** and ran to the door.*

  Answer: Yes, it does.

TOP TIP ⭐

Think! Have you heard or used the phrase before? What did it mean then? Can you link it to your own experience?

NOW YOU TRY!

His breathing was fast as he scanned the traffic for the school bus. Toby was beginning to think he was out of luck!

What does the phrase **out of luck** tell us about Toby's thoughts?

Toby is thinking ....

....

....

20

EXPLAIN PHRASE MEANINGS 2

❶ Sometimes phrases don't mean exactly what they say and you have to work out what the words are trying to tell you. These phrases are often used for comparisons.

Helen is like a snail when she walks to school.

Q: What do the words *like a snail* tell us about Helen?

Good answer: *She walks very slowly.*

❷ How do you work out what the words are trying to tell you?

- We often use similes to compare two different things.

- In the example, we know that Helen is being compared to a snail because of the word *like*. We need to decide which features of a snail are important.

- We know that Helen is walking and we also know that snails move very slowly, so this is a big clue. Helen must walk **very slowly** on the way to school.

TOP TIP ⭐

Similes use 'like' or 'as' to compare things.

❸ Metaphors make comparisons between two different things that have something in common.

I need lots of sleep at night time, but my big brother is a night owl.

Q: What does the phrase *night owl* mean?

HINT! 💡

We know the brother isn't an owl, he's a boy. What are the characteristics of an owl that might give you a clue?

Good answer: *He is like a night owl because he likes to be awake at night.*

TOP TIP ⭐

If something 'is' or 'was' something else, it might be a **metaphor**.

NOW YOU TRY!

The sound of the engine starting was music to his ears and straight away he felt relieved.

What does the phrase *music to his ears* mean?

....

QUICK QUIZ: EXPLAIN PHRASE MEANINGS

1 Read the text.

Layla was short of time. She knew she had to get to the station in twenty minutes, but she wasn't ready. She still had to pack her bag and tidy her room, and she was getting in a muddle.

a) Which word is closest in meaning to **short of time**?

Tick **one**.

quick ☐

early ☐

rushed ☐

slow ☐

b) **Find** and **copy** the group of words which means that Layla wasn't very organised.

....

2 Read the text.

We're organising a surprise party for Joe, so it's important we keep him in the dark about what's happening on Friday. If he finds out, we've blown it! We don't want to have a last-minute change of plan.

Match the **phrases** on the left to the correct **meaning** on the right.

(1 keep him in the dark)

(A ruined a plan)

(2 blown it)

(B doing something just before it is needed)

(3 last-minute)

(C don't tell someone a secret)

3 Read the text.

Last night, Harriet was ready to go on stage for her trumpet solo, but she got cold feet when she saw how many people were watching, and she couldn't do it.

Tick the correct meaning of **got cold feet**.

was late ☐   felt tired ☐

became nervous ☐   felt excited ☐

4 Read the text.

'I've been as busy as a bee today,' said Rashid. 'I've done all my homework, tidied my room, and fed my pets. Now I'm going to take some time out and watch my favourite programme on TV.'

a) Why do you think Rashid uses the words **as busy as a bee**?

Because he has ...

Tick **one**.

… worked in a very small space. ☐

… done lots of things quickly. ☐

… fed his pets. ☐

… finished one important thing. ☐

b) **Find** and **copy** the group of words which mean that Rashid is now going to relax.

....

....

Wow, you're making great progress!

→ EXPLAIN PHRASE MEANINGS →

EXPLAIN HOW WORDS AFFECT MEANING

1 **Some words are chosen to create an effect. They can tell you more about a character, object, setting or mood.**

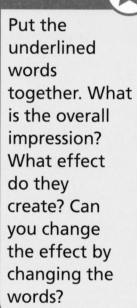

The sinister ship creaked and groaned eerily as it drifted through the grey, gloomy sea.

Q: **Find** and **copy two** words that suggest the mood was uneasy.

Good answer: 1. *sinister*   2. *eerily*

2 **How do you identify words that affect meaning?**

- **Look for words** that tell you more about an object, character, setting or mood and <u>underline</u> them.

- The **adjectives** and **adverbs** are important in the example: *sinister, eerily, grey* and *gloomy*.

- **Think about the effect these words create** when we put them together.

  - Without them, we just have an ordinary ship drifting on the sea. When we add these extra words, it creates a different effect.

  - If you change these words, you can change the meaning completely.

    E.g. *The **beautiful** ship creaked and groaned **quietly** as it drifted through the **blue**, **sparkling** sea.*

NOW YOU TRY!

Raj was new to the school. He was a pleasant child who was friendly towards others. He was also very clever and got all the answers right in class.

Find and **copy two** words which show that Raj was a nice person.

....

....

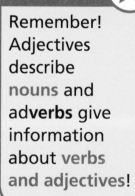

EXPLAIN HOW PHRASES AFFECT MEANING

❶ **We often use phrases to give more information. They can change the meaning of a sentence, create a picture or explain feelings or a situation more clearly.**

Evelyn couldn't believe what the Prince was saying. The words were like a dagger to her heart.

Q: How does Evelyn feel about what the Prince was saying to her?

Good answer: *She is very upset/hurt by his words.*

❷ **How do you find and understand phrases that affect meaning?**

- **Similes** and **metaphors** are often used in phrases. It's your job to **understand what they mean**.

- Look at the phrase *like a dagger to her heart*. This **simile** is about words that are said to Evelyn. If someone has a dagger in their heart, they are clearly in pain.

- This **simile creates a vivid picture** and shows that Evelyn was very hurt by the words she heard, not just a little bit upset.

TOP TIP ⭐

Remember: **Similes** have **'like'** or **'as'** to compare things.

If something **'is'** or **'was'** something else, it might be a **metaphor**.

NOW YOU TRY!

Waves rose up like mountains, battering everything in their way. They crashed persistently around the boat.

Which phrase tells us that the waves were big?

....

....

HINT! 💡

Remember, you are looking for a phrase, not a single word.

QUICK QUIZ: EXPLAIN HOW WORDS AND PHRASES AFFECT MEANING

1 Read the sentence. Then look at the words in the box. Can you use them in the correct order to change the meaning of the sentence?

The small dogs barked loudly in the garden.

> quietly   big

The .... dogs barked

.... in the garden.

2 Read the text. Complete the table with the correct words.

People were talking noisily in the big, old train station. They were running quickly along the busy platforms.

Words about the train station/platforms	
Words about what the people were doing	

3 Match the words to the correct definition.

1 Metaphor	A a word that gives information about a verb or adjective
2 Adverb	B a word used to describe something or somebody
3 Simile	C a direct comparison saying something really is another thing
4 Adjective	D a comparison of one thing to another using 'like' or 'as'

4 Read the text.

Guy was exhausted after the party. When he went to bed, he was out like a light!

a) Tick the correct words to complete the sentence:

Guy went to sleep ...

quickly ☐   in the dark ☐   quietly ☐

b) Which one of these sentences explains **why** we use *out like a light* to describe how someone goes to sleep?

Tick **one**.

You turn out a light at night time. ☐

When you turn out a light, it goes dark quickly. ☐

You can turn a light on and off whenever you want to. ☐

5 Read the text.

You really should go to see the new art exhibition in town. Some of the paintings are out of this world!

a) Which of these words is closest in meaning to the **phrase** *out of this world*? Tick **one**.

amazing ☐   expensive ☐

ordinary ☐   traditional ☐

b) Why do you think *out of this world* has this meaning?

....

....

....

....

Wow, you're making great progress!

FINISH

→ EXPLAIN HOW WORDS AND PHRASES AFFECT MEANING →

CHECK OUT INFORMATION!
FIND FACTS 1

1 **You may be asked questions which require a simple one-word response.**

Ivy's grandad left school when he was fourteen. He got a job at a car factory and he loved it! He worked there for sixty years!

Q: How old was Ivy's grandad when he left school?

Good answer: *fourteen*

2 **How do you find the correct facts?**

- Remember to **read the question carefully**.

- **Scan the text for important information.** The example question asks *How old …*, so you're looking for an age, or number. There are two numbers in the text: *fourteen* and *sixty*.

- **Read around the chosen number** to check that it relates to the **correct information**. Does it answer the question you've been asked?

  - The example question includes the word *school*, so the correct answer is *fourteen*, not *sixty*.

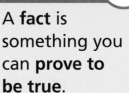

TOP TIP

A **fact** is something you can **prove to be true**.

TOP TIP

There may be several numbers in a text, so always read carefully to check what the numbers relate to.

NOW YOU TRY!

The Eiffel Tower was opened in 1889. It took two years to build. It is 324 metres tall.

a) When was the Eiffel Tower opened?

  ....

b) How tall is the Eiffel Tower?

  ....

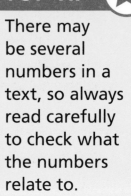

28

FIND FACTS 2

1 **You need to find true information in a text to help you answer questions. You might have to choose from different answers which are all quite similar.**

Most snakes eat insects, rodents, birds and frogs.

Q: Which of the following sentences is true? Tick **one**.

Snakes only eat insects. ☐ Snakes eat lots of different things. ☐

All snakes eat frogs. ☐ Snakes only eat mammals and birds. ☐

Good answer: *Snakes eat lots of different things.*

2 **How do you find true information in a text?**

- **Read the question.** What information do you need?

- **Scan the text for factual information** such as numbers, names, dates, or other key **nouns**.

- **Compare the answer options to the text.** Can you identify any that are wrong or inaccurate? E.g. the text says *Most snakes* so the option that says *All snakes* must be wrong. The text lists several things they eat, so the *Snakes **only** eat* sentences must be inaccurate.

- **Look at the remaining answer options.** Which one is true? In the example, *Snakes eat lots of different things* is the only one which can be true!

TOP TIP ⭐

Underline any important information in the text.

TOP TIP ⭐

If you see words such as *think, believe, feel*, you are reading someone's **opinion**, rather than a **fact**.

NOW YOU TRY!

Elephants have a slow pulse rate of about 27 beats per minute. They can live for up to 70 years in the wild, but only about 40 years in captivity. A female elephant is pregnant for 22 months.

Which of the following sentences is true? Tick **one**.

Elephants have a fast pulse rate. ☐

Elephants live longer in a zoo. ☐

Elephants live longer in the wild. ☐

Elephants are pregnant for less than a year. ☐

In captivity means I'm kept in a zoo.

29

FIND DETAILS 1

1 **You may have to** find and copy certain information to show you have understood the text.

Working in the mines was back-breaking, but factory jobs were dangerous too. Factories were often in very big buildings.

Q: **Find** and **copy two** different words that show how difficult jobs were in Victorian England.

Good answer: 1. *back-breaking*, 2. *dangerous*

2 **How do you know which** words to copy?

- **Read the question carefully** to find the **key word** you are being asked to find information about e.g. *jobs*. Are there other words that mean the same thing? Yes – the word *working* in the text is also used to talk about jobs.

- Next, find the **key adjective in the question**, e.g. *difficult*. Here you need to look for adjectives that are close in meaning to *difficult*.

TOP TIP

Find and copy means that you can copy the words for an answer straight from the text.

NOW YOU TRY!

We made a picnic to take to the beach when our cousin Sally came to visit. Sally is vegetarian so we took cheese and salad sandwiches, and lots of drinks and fruit. She is very sporty, so we took some bats and a ball.

Find and **copy one** word that means Sally doesn't eat meat.

....

HINT!

Look at the text around an unfamiliar word to see if you can use any clues to help work out the meaning.

TOP TIP

Follow the question exactly – does it ask you to copy **one word**, **two words**, or a **phrase**? Make sure you answer with the correct number of things.

FIND DETAILS 2

1 **You may need to** write a sentence **to answer a question** using information **in the text.**

There was a week to go before Jack's skiing trip. He was excited but also nervous. What if he couldn't ski? What if he hurt himself?

Q: Why does Jack have mixed feelings about his skiing trip?

Good answer: *Jack has mixed feelings* **because** *he's excited about it but also worried that he won't be able to do it, or might get injured.*

2 **How do you** construct your sentence?

- **Read the question** and **identify the key words**. These will tell you what information you need to give. The key words in the example question are *Why* and *mixed feelings*. You need to give a reason for Jack feeling more than one thing.

- **Read the text carefully**. The example question asks **why** Jack feels the way he does, so you need to find the part of the text that **explains** how he feels and see if there is a **reason** given for this.

- Use *because* in your answer to give the reason.

- **Try to use your own words** as much as possible, but you can pick out words from the question and the text to help you: *Jack has* **mixed** *feelings* **because** *he's* **excited** ....

TOP TIP ⭐

If the question asks **Why …?** you need to answer with **because ….**

NOW YOU TRY!

Tim's mum was cross. She had a new mobile phone, but it stopped working after a week. She had to go back to the shop and change it.

Why was Tim's mum unhappy with her new phone?

....

....

QUICK QUIZ: FIND FACTS; FIND DETAILS

1 Read the text.

Blue Whale Fact File

Blue whales are the largest animals on earth. They can grow up to 30 metres long and weigh 150 tonnes or more. However, they eat tiny food called krill. If they are in danger they can swim at up to 25 miles an hour, but they usually swim at around 5 miles an hour.

Complete the table with information from the text.

Maximum length	
Maximum weight	
What they eat	
Maximum speed	
Usual speed	

2 Read the sentences below about giraffes. Can you match the **beginnings** and **endings**?

1 Giraffes are the tallest …

A … 5.5 metres!

2 They can grow up to …

B … leaves and twigs.

3 Giraffes eat …

C … 30 years.

4 They live for about …

D … animals on land.

③ Read the text and answer the questions which follow.

Emma Watson is a famous British actress and model. You probably know her as Hermione Granger in the 'Harry Potter' films. She spent ten years working in the eight films, from 2001 to 2011. Since then she has done lots of different things, including acting in the film 'Beauty and the Beast' and completing an English degree.

a) What made Emma Watson famous? Tick **one**.

Being a model. ☐   Being an actress. ☐

b) How long did she spend being Hermione Granger? Tick **one**.

Ten years. ☐   Eight years ☐

c) What has she done since then? Tick **one**.

Read lots of books. ☐

She's done more acting and studying. ☐

④ Read the text and complete the sentences with information from the text.

Michael Morpurgo is a very successful author who was born in 1943 in Hertfordshire. He has written over 100 books! One of his most famous books is 'War Horse'. He was a teacher before he became a writer.

a) Michael hasn't always been a writer. He used to be a

....

b) Some writers only produce a few books, but there

are .... by

Michael Morpurgo!

c) .... is one of his best-known books.

 *Wow, you're making great progress!*

→ FIND FACTS → FIND DETAILS →

IDENTIFY FACT AND OPINION

1 **Recognising the difference between a** fact **and an** opinion **is an important skill.** Facts are true information **but** opinions are people's views.

The Burj Khalifa tower in Dubai is the tallest building in the world. It is over 828 metres tall. I think it's amazing and very beautiful.

Q: Tick the correct box to show whether each of the following statements is a **fact** or an **opinion**.

	Fact	Opinion
1. The Burj Khalifa tower in Dubai is the tallest building in the world.		
2. It is over 828 metres tall.		
3. It's amazing and very beautiful.		

Good answer: 1. *Fact*; 2. *Fact*; 3. *Opinion*

2 **How do you work out whether you are reading a** fact **or an** opinion?

- **A fact is something that you can prove.**

  You can measure the Burj Khalifa and prove that it is over 828 metres tall. You can also compare this to the heights of other buildings in the world to prove it is the tallest.

- **An opinion is someone's view.**

  You cannot prove that something is beautiful. One person may think something is beautiful, but the same thing may be ugly to another person.

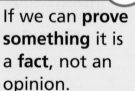

TOP TIP

If we can **prove something** it is a **fact**, not an opinion.

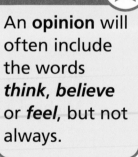

TOP TIP

An **opinion** will often include the words *think*, *believe* or *feel*, but not always.

NOW YOU TRY!

Warwick Castle is over 1,000 years old. It's open to the public every day of the week. I think it's interesting to learn about the history of England by visiting places like this.

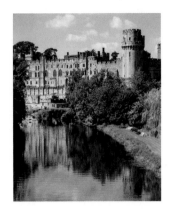

Tick the correct box to show whether each of the following statements is a **fact** or an **opinion**.

	Fact	Opinion
Warwick Castle is over 1,000 years old.		
It is open to the public every day of the week.		
It's interesting to learn about the history of England by visiting places like this.		

HINT!

Check the text to see if the sentences are preceded by any opinion words.

TOP TIP

It may help to **underline** the **opinion words** within the text.

PRACTISE AGAIN!

The Junior Premier League has some of the best young football players from all over the country. In my view, it's good for young players to have challenging games. They sometimes have to travel a long way for their games.

Tick the correct box to show whether each of the following statements is a **fact** or an **opinion**.

	Fact	Opinion
The Junior Premier League has some of the best young football players from all over the country.		
It's good for young players to have challenging games.		
They sometimes have to travel a long way for their games.		

IDENTIFY TRUE AND FALSE

❶ You may be asked to say if a statement is true or false. To do this, you need to read the text carefully to look for clues. You may have to look for key words in the text that are similar in meaning to the words in the question.

Sir Mo Farah is one of the UK's greatest athletes. He won two Olympic Gold medals in 2012 and two more in 2016, in both the 5,000 m and 10,000 m races. He has retired from track racing now and runs marathons.

Q: Tick **one** box in each row to show whether each statement is **true** or **false**.

	True	False
1. Mo Farah won three gold medals in total.		
2. He doesn't race on tracks now.		
3. He only won medals for 5,000 m races.		

Good answer: 1. *False*; 2. *True*; 3. *False*

❷ How do you work out whether something is true or false?

TOP TIP ⭐

Look for evidence to prove or disprove the statement. If you can't find anything wrong with the statement, then it must be true!

- **Look at the text.** Use **skimming** and **scanning** to find the part that contains the answer. For the first statement in the table, you need to look for information about medals.

- When you find the correct place, e.g. the word *medal* in the text, **read the text around it carefully.**

- Look for **parts of the statement** that don't match the text.

- For example, in this text it says that Mo Farah *won* **two** *medals in 2012 and* **two** *more in 2016.* This means he won **four** medals in total, so the statement saying he won only **three** medals is wrong, or false.

TOP TIP ⭐

You might see similar words, but this doesn't mean the statement is true. Check the meaning of the text carefully.

NOW YOU TRY!

Adele is a very famous English singer and songwriter. She has sold millions of records and is very rich. Her album 21 has sold over 31 million copies worldwide.

Tick **one** box in each row to show whether each statement is **true** or **false**.

	True	False
Adele is only famous in the UK.		
She is from Wales.		
She has made a lot of money.		

TOP TIP ★

Look for **words with similar meanings** to help you.

PRACTISE AGAIN!

Colchester is one of the oldest towns in Britain. It is in the east of England. It was a very important Roman city, and later the Normans built a castle which you can visit today. There is also an interesting zoo, which is a popular tourist attraction.

Tick **one** box in each row to show whether each statement is **true** or **false**.

	True	False
Colchester is an ancient place.		
The Normans used the Roman castle.		
People only visit because of the history.		

QUICK QUIZ: IDENTIFY FACT AND OPINION; IDENTIFY TRUE AND FALSE

1 Read the statements. **Tick** the ones you could prove. **Underline** the ones that are an opinion.

A
> The Indian Ocean is 74 million km².

☐

B
> I think it's important to protect wildlife.

☐

C
> Some of the most beautiful animals in the world live in Africa.

☐

2 Read the facts and opinions. Match them to the correct animal by writing a letter on each answer line.

FACT ....
OPINION ....

FACT ....
OPINION ....

FACT ....
OPINION ....

A
> These animals have brightly coloured feathers.

B
> It would be scary if one of them chased you!

C
> These animals are fish. They live in rivers in South America.

D
> I wouldn't like to go swimming with one!

E
> These animals can weigh up to 2,500 kg.

F
> I think they look very beautiful.

3 Read the quiz. Use the text to help you work out whether each statement is **true** or **false**.

Shark facts!

Sharks are amazing animals! They have been on earth for over 400 million years, so they are one of the oldest animals. Some people think that all sharks will attack you, but this isn't true. Lots of sharks don't attack people, and some are very shy.

Their sense of smell is excellent, and they have very good vision in the dark as well. Instead of bones they have cartilage, which is softer.

What do you know about sharks?

		True	False
a	All sharks are dangerous.	☐	☐
b	Sharks have an excellent sense of smell.	☐	☐
c	Sharks don't have bones.	☐	☐
d	Sharks can't see very well in the dark.	☐	☐

4 Read the text about sharks again. Find **two** more facts about sharks.

1 ....

2 ....

   *Wow, you're making great progress!*

→ IDENTIFY FACT AND OPINION → IDENTIFY TRUE AND FALSE →

CHECK OUT SUMMARISING!
ORDER EVENTS

❶ You might have to order events to show you understand what has happened.

The train chugged through the countryside, puffing out billowing clouds of smoke.

All at once there was a bang. The train ground to a halt, then there was silence. Tom was rooted to his seat. Surely they hadn't tracked him down? He'd tried to cover his tracks. Panic rose inside him and he knew he had to do something.

With a sudden surge of energy, he opened the carriage door, leapt out, then ran blindly into the surrounding woods. He tripped over something on the ground, but ignored the pain as he dragged himself up. He stopped to catch his breath. Suddenly a hand clamped onto his shoulder.

'Got you!' a rough voice said.

Q: Number the sentences 1–4 to show the order in which they happened.

A   Tom jumped off the train. ☐

B   Tom got caught. ☐

C   Tom was sitting on the train. ☐

D   Tom heard a bang. ☐

Good answer: *A 3; B 4; C 1; D 2*

❷ How do you order events within a story?

- Read all the statements (or sentences) in the question first.
- Check **how many statements** there are to order, then **refer back to the text** and **underline** the same number of events.
- **Match the statements** with the **order of events** in the text.
- Always **check your order!**

> **TOP TIP** ⭐
>
> It may help to **number the sentences or phrases** you've underlined in the text so you can **match them to the statements/ sentences** in the question.

- **Find clues** in the words and phrases in the statements and **identify the meanings.**

- **Match the meanings** to the text.

- Remember, you may not find exactly the same words so look for words with a **similar meaning.**

NOW YOU TRY!

Re-read the text on page 40.

Number the sentences 1–5 to show the order in which they happened.

Tom opened the door of the train.

Tom couldn't move.

Someone touched his shoulder.

The train was moving.

Tom started to panic.

PRACTISE AGAIN!

Tom gasped with fear as the man pulled him back. Before he turned around, he put his hand inside his pocket. The SIM card was still there. Should he throw it away? There wasn't time. He turned around to see two masked men looking at him.

'Where is it?' shouted the one who had grabbed him.

'I haven't got it.' Tom replied, hoping to buy a bit more time.

Number the sentences 1–4 to show the order in which they happened.

Tom feels the SIM card in his pocket.

The man asks Tom a question.

Tom sees two men wearing masks.

The man pulls Tom back.

SUMMARISE PARAGRAPHS

1 **You may be asked to** explain the main facts and themes **of a text in just** a few words. **This is called summarising. Sometimes you will be given all the information and just need to** match it up.

What is ice hockey?

Ice hockey is a game of speed, skill and strength. It was first played in Canada on frozen ponds. It's a team game that is played on ice.

How do you play?

Ice hockey is played in teams of six players. Each player has a stick and the aim is to use the stick to hit a puck (a rubber disk) into the opponent's net.

What do you need to play?

You need lots of equipment to play. You need ice skates and protective gear, such as a helmet, pads and gloves.

Q: Draw lines to match each section to its main content summary.

TOP TIP ★

You don't have to understand every word. You only have to **understand the main idea** of each **paragraph.**

Section

1 What is ice hockey?

2 How do you play?

3 What do you need to play?

Main content summary

A Information about teams and rules

B Information about what equipment you need

C A description of the sport

Good answer: *1 C; 2 A; 3 B*

❷ How do you match information?

- **Read the instructions carefully** so that you know what to do.

- Start with the **easiest to match**.

- Look for any **key words and clues** that will help you.

  For example, statement 2 in the text on page 42 is about **how** you **play** and statement 1 in the *Main content summary* column mentions **rules**. This gives you a big clue that these two parts must be linked.

- **Read the text** so that you understand the general meaning.

- **Check your answers**.

NOW YOU TRY!

Read the rest of the text about ice hockey.

How to get started

You need to be able to skate and not be scared of falling over. Find the nearest ice rink and join the local training sessions.

Professional games

Watch a professional game to experience the excitement and speed of the action. It will also help you to understand the rules.

Hazards

Ice hockey is a contact sport. You must be prepared for a few bumps and bruises! Ice is a hard surface to land on!

Draw lines to match each section to its main content summary.

Section

| 1 How to get started |

| 2 Professional games |

| 3 Hazards |

Main content summary

| A Injuries you might get from playing ice hockey. |

| B What to do if you are keen to play ice hockey. |

| C Learn by watching. |

❶ You may be asked to choose from a list of summaries for a text. You will need to understand what the whole text is about.

Storm Ophelia brought strong winds of around 80 mph to the UK, causing chaos and damage. There were lots of weather warnings, and over 200 homes in Wales were without power for a long time.

Q: Which of the following would be the most suitable summary of the whole text?

Tick **one**.

Stormy waters

Ophelia's day out

A storm is coming

A storm strikes

Good answer: *A storm strikes*

❷ How do you summarise the whole text?

- **Read the text carefully** to understand what it is about.

- **Pick out the main points** and **important information**.

- **Read each of the summaries** and work out which ones don't work.

- **Decide which one** fits best.

  E.g. we know that the text above is about a **storm**, not an **outing** or **water**. It is written in the **past tense**, so it has already happened and is not **coming**. This leaves just one correct summary.

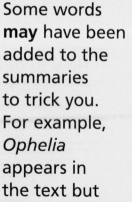

TOP TIP

Be careful! Some words **may** have been added to the summaries to trick you. For example, *Ophelia* appears in the text but *Ophelia's day out* = incorrect answer!

NOW YOU TRY!

Horace the hedgehog was in a spot of trouble. He had become wedged in a fence as he tried to get out of the park, and he couldn't free himself. Luckily, a passer-by saw him and helped him to escape. Horace was a bit scared, but otherwise unharmed.

Which of the following would be the most suitable summary of the whole text?

Tick **one**.

Horace's exciting adventure

A difficult rescue

A lucky escape

Horace is harmed

HINT!

There will probably be relevant words in each summary, so don't just guess because you recognise a word.

PRACTISE AGAIN!

Tia was walking home from school when she saw something glistening in the sunlight. As she got closer, it began to move. It slithered across the path in front of her like a snake. She crouched down, leaning closer to the strange-looking creature. Suddenly, it spoke ...

Which of the following would be the most suitable summary of the whole text?

Tick **one**.

A snake on the loose

An unusual find

Tia's new friend

School days

1 Read the text.

Leah was sitting quietly in her bedroom when the phone rang. She heard her brother answer it.

'I've told you not to call me here!' he shouted.

Leah was worried. Why was he so angry?

Suddenly, she heard the front door slam. She looked out of the window and saw her brother cycling away towards the park.

Number the sentences 1–5 to show the order in which they happened.

The front door slams. ☐

The phone rings. ☐

Leah is worried. ☐

Leah's brother is angry. ☐

Leah's brother goes out on his bike. ☐

2 Read the notes. Write the letter of each note so that the instructions are in the correct order.

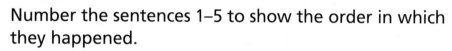

A water it and put it in sunlight

D take a plant pot

B put the seed in the hole

E make a hole in the soil

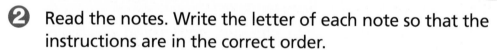

C fill the plant pot with soil

To grow a plant you need to:

1. ....

2. ....

3. ....

4. ....

5. ....

3 Match the **headings** below with paragraphs 1–4 by writing the correct letter on each line.

A **What do I need to make it?**

B **What will live in it?**

C **Where do I put it?**

D **About bug hotels**

1 ....

Have you ever seen a bug hotel? These can be a great shelter for all sorts of animals. They're easy and fun to make.

2 ....

Animals such as bees, ladybirds, woodlice and even toads might make it their home!

3 ....

You can make one using natural materials such as straw, dry grass and bits of wood.

4 ....

You should put it somewhere quiet, and try not to disturb it too much.

4 Read the text.

We visited a palace when we were on holiday last year. I thought it was going to be boring, but actually I loved it! The rooms were so beautiful, and there were lots of interesting paintings. I enjoyed walking round the gardens, too.

a) Which of the following would be the best summary of the text? Tick **one**.

A bad day out ☐

A visit to an art gallery ☐

An interesting palace ☐

A walk in the gardens ☐

b) Which of the following sentences is true? Tick **one**.

She didn't think she would like it, but she did. ☐

She thought she would like it, but she didn't. ☐

Wow, you're making great progress!

→ ORDER EVENTS → SUMMARISE PARAGRAPHS →
SUMMARISE THE WHOLE TEXT →

FINISH

1 Sometimes the **message of the text is hidden. You have to be a detective and look at the clues to work out** what the text is trying to tell you.

Lots of people love fireworks. They're beautiful and exciting to look at. However, they can be dangerous. They contain a lot of gunpowder and it's risky to handle them. Every year, some people are badly injured. It's a very good idea to go to an organised display instead. The crowd is a safe distance from the explosions, and the fireworks are only handled by people who have been trained.

Q: What is the text trying to tell the reader?

Good answer: *The text is saying that fireworks are dangerous and that people should go to organised displays instead of handling them themselves.*

2 How do you **find messages** in the text?

- Some texts are written to **persuade you** to think or behave in a certain way; or **to warn you** about something; or to **give you advice**.

- Often you will need to **read the whole text** to understand the exact message.

- In the example, the words *dangerous* and *risky* tell us that fireworks are not safe. The words *It's a very good idea ...* tell us that this is advice and should probably be followed.

TOP TIP ⭐

Look carefully at the words that are used. Are they warning you, persuading you, or giving you advice?

NOW YOU TRY!

High tides are common during the summer months. These can be dangerous to walkers and you should take care not to get caught out. Avoid walking on the sea wall.

What advice does the text give and why?

....

....

FIND THE MESSAGE 2

❶ **Sometimes the aim of a story is to teach you a lesson or to persuade you to think in a certain way.**

Taryn had cried 'Wolf!' so many times when there wasn't a wolf anywhere, that now none of the villagers listened to him. They had responded to his cries many times and rushed out to rescue him, only to be laughed at when Taryn said he'd fooled them. But this time, when there really was an angry-looking wolf snarling at him, no one came to his rescue.

Q: What is the message or moral of this story?

Good answer: *The story tells me that if you tell lies, no one will believe you when you really need them to.*

❷ **How do you find the moral or message of a story?**

TOP TIP ⭐

A **moral** is a lesson in a story about the right way to behave.

- **Break down the story** into separate parts and **summarise each event**. What do the characters do, say or think? Look at the actions and reactions. E.g. Taryn has tricked the villagers and laughed at them many times = **action**. The villagers have stopped listening to him, so no one was there when he really needed help = **reaction**.

- Does the **outcome of the story** change because of what the main character does or doesn't do? If so, can we learn a lesson from this? E.g. if they hadn't been tricked so often the villagers would have helped = a different outcome. **Message** = tell lies and people won't help you.

TOP TIP ⭐

Look at the **actions** of the character. What are the **reactions**? What do you learn?

NOW YOU TRY!

'Look how high I can climb!' shouted Oliver. Oliver's father shouted to him, telling him to be careful, but Oliver ignored his warnings.

All of a sudden, Oliver started to wobble and soon completely lost his balance as he tumbled out of the tree onto the hard ground.

What is the message of this story?

....

....

QUICK QUIZ: FIND THE MESSAGE

1 Read the text.

Talia was really happy. For her birthday, she had been given a lot of money, and she was looking forward to spending it. There were lots of clothes she wanted, and new shoes.

She waited until the weekend and then went out shopping with her friends. She came back with lots of bags full of lovely clothes and shoes for her holiday.

Soon, it was her dad's birthday. Talia realised that she hadn't saved any money to buy him a present. She felt sad, and angry with herself.

In the end, she decided to take some of her new clothes back to the shop. With the money she got back, she bought a present for her dad.

There are two important messages in the story.

Tick **two** of the sentences below to explain the messages.

You feel happy when you get clothes for your birthday. ☐

It's fun spending money on yourself. ☐

Don't spend all your money in one go. ☐

You should go shopping with your parents. ☐

It's nice to get presents, but it's better to give them. ☐

❷ Read the text.

A new skate park will be built in the town soon. It's a popular idea, as it will give teenagers and young people somewhere to meet where they can do a fun activity.

However, when the builders started digging up the ground, they found some very old objects from the Bronze Age. Now some people think that they shouldn't build on the site in case there are more objects in the ground that could tell historians about life in the Bronze Age.

Now read the statements below.

Decide if each statement is **'For'** building the skate park (it's saying building the skate park would be a good thing) or **'Against'** building the skate park (it's saying building the skate park is a bad idea).

Tick the correct column for each statement.

	For	Against
The skate park will be a good place for young people to meet.		
There might be more things to find in the ground.		
Historians can find out about the Bronze Age from the objects found there.		
Skateboarding is a fun thing to do.		

Wow, you're making great progress!

→ FIND THE MESSAGE →

1 **You need to be able to make inferences. This means reading 'between the lines' to find answers that are hidden in the text.**

Things weren't going well and they were running out of time. Martha stamped her feet and raised her voice. The rest of the group had to start working together before it was too late.

Q: How does Martha feel?

Tick **one**.

happy ☐   angry ☐   sad ☐   shy ☐

Good answer: *angry*

2 **How do you work out (*infer*) how a character feels by looking at their actions/what they do?**

- Ask yourself **why** you are told something. **What** message is the text trying to get across?

- E.g. *Martha stamped her feet and raised her voice.* You are told this for a **reason**. What picture does it create in your mind?

- In stories, **actions** (what people do) often **tell us how someone is feeling**. Look for **action words** (**verbs**). Do these give you any clues?

TOP TIP ⭐

Try putting yourself in the place of the character. If you stamped your feet, how would you be feeling?

NOW YOU TRY!

Sangit looked across at his mother. His lips started quivering and his eyes filled with tears.

How does Sangit feel?

Tick **one**.

bored ☐   jealous ☐   happy ☐   sad ☐

MAKE INFERENCES 2

1 You can also work out **how a character feels** by what they **say** or how they say it.

'I don't want to go in there,' James said hesitantly. 'My legs are shaking.'

Q: James is scared. Give **two** pieces of evidence from the text which shows this.

Good answer: *James is scared **because** he says his legs are shaking and he is hesitating when he says he doesn't want to go in.*

2 How do you **infer feelings** through speech?

- **What you say** and **how you say it** often tells people **how you feel**.

- Look for **adverbs** to help you identify feelings. *Hesitantly* = not feeling very confident.

- **Look for other clues too** and make sure you give the correct number of pieces of evidence asked for in the question!

- **Put all the clues together.** James says he doesn't want to go in + he speaks hesitatingly + he says his legs are shaking = he is scared.

TOP TIP ⭐

Most **inference questions** will ask you **to give evidence** for your answer.

Evidence is the part of the text that **proves** your answer. Look for the **clue words** in the text!

TOP TIP ⭐

Use the word **because** if you are asked **to give evidence** for your answer.

NOW YOU TRY!

'Yes!' Karen shouted loudly, bouncing around the living room like an over-enthusiastic puppy. 'I've always wanted to go there.'

How does Karen feel? Give **one** piece of evidence from the text.

....

....

....

....

LOOK AT ALL THE CLUES

❶ It's very important to look at <u>ALL</u> of the clues. Sometimes a character doesn't tell you how they really feel. Instead they show you with clues.

Janine sat at the table listening to the conversation around her. She was suddenly aware that all eyes were on her.

'Well?' said her grandmother. 'What do you think? Can Lauren share your room?'

'Of course she can. That would make me very happy.' muttered Janine, ripping her napkin into small pieces under the table.

Q: How does Janine feel about Lauren sharing her room? Explain your answer using evidence from the text.

Good answer: *Janine is not very happy about it because she is ripping her napkin up. This shows that she might be frustrated or angry.*

❷ **How do you decide** which clues are important?

- Do you say things you don't really mean? A character might do the same!

  E.g. Janine says that she is *very happy* for Lauren to share her room, but ripping a napkin into small pieces = a sign of frustration or anger. Janine mutters when she speaks, which suggests she may not be happy, even though she says she is.

TOP TIP ⭐

Actions and **speech** may **not match**. Often the actions speak louder than the words.

NOW YOU TRY!

'Ready?' asked the instructor.

'Yes, I can't wait,' I replied convincingly. 'I'm really looking forward to this.'

As I stood waiting for my turn, my hands were shaking and sweat was running down my forehead. I was pacing up and down and could feel my heart in my throat.

How does the character feel? Give **one** piece of evidence from the text.

....

....

INFER THOUGHTS

❶ You might be asked to infer what a character is thinking.

'I'll have the special pasta dish, please,' said the restaurant inspector.

Carl hoped that the inspector hadn't noticed the smell of burning pasta coming from the kitchen. His heart started to pound and he could feel himself beginning to panic.

'Would you prefer a salad?' he asked.

Q: Why does Carl start to panic? Give **two** pieces of evidence from the text.

Good answer: *The restaurant inspector wants to try the pasta dish. There is a smell of burning pasta and so Carl is worried that the inspector will find out he has burnt the food.*

TOP TIP

Sometimes the **thoughts of a character** are stated clearly in the text, but sometimes you have to **infer** what they are thinking.

❷ How do you make inferences about thoughts?

 Actions often show you something about the **thoughts** of a character.

 Ask yourself: **Why** does the character do that? **What** are they thinking when they do that?

NOW YOU TRY!

The whole shelf full of antique china came crashing down and smashed on the floor. Jack's eyes widened and he shook his head.

What is Jack thinking? Explain your answer.

....

....

TOP TIP

If you find this difficult, ask yourself what you would think in the same situation. Then think about the character. Would they think in the same way as you?

FIND HIDDEN MOTIVES

❶ **You might need** to find the hidden motive **in a text. This means** the reason why someone does something.

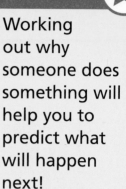

TOP TIP ⭐

Working out why someone does something will help you to predict what will happen next!

Isaac knew that the activity was going to be difficult. He'd tried building a raft once before, but it had been a disaster. He looked around the room and spotted Oliver, whose dad was an engineer. Isaac moved closer to Oliver.

Q: Why do you think Isaac moved closer to Oliver?

Good answer: *Isaac finds raft-building difficult and might be hoping that Oliver will help him.*

❷ **How do you work out the motives in a story?**

- **Read all the facts.** What do you already know? Isaac's last raft was a *disaster*; Oliver's dad is an *engineer*. (Engineers are good at working out how to build things.)

- **Connect the facts.** How are they linked?
  Oliver's dad is an engineer → Oliver might be good at raft building → Isaac needs help → Oliver might be able to help him → Isaac moves closer to Oliver.

- **What do the facts tell you?**
  By moving closer to Oliver, Isaac will be more likely to talk to him. This means he might be able to get some advice or tips.

TOP TIP ⭐

Connecting facts is like doing a jigsaw puzzle. Put all the pieces together and you get the full picture!

NOW YOU TRY!

Toby kicked the stolen bag further under the table so that it ended up next to Dylan. No one noticed. Toby knew that Marty would come looking for the bag soon and didn't fancy being on the receiving end of his fiery temper. He approached Marty and, with a sickly smile, asked if he could help him.

Why did Toby kick the stolen bag next to Dylan?

....

....

❸ **Did you see?** You need to connect the facts in the story about Toby and Marty to find the hidden meaning: *Marty will look for the bag → Marty has a bad temper → Toby wanted to blame someone else → Toby kicked the bag next to Dylan so Marty would think Dylan stole the bag.*

PRACTISE AGAIN!

Lucy read the list of players for the netball match again. She wasn't down as a reserve. She sighed. She'd really been hoping that she'd be able to play. Sally, Mia and Ella were all on the list.

She looked up as she saw Ella coming down the corridor. Ella was coughing and suddenly, Lucy had an idea.

'Ella, are you ok?' asked Lucy. 'You look really ill! Shall I take you to the nurse?'

a) Why does Lucy tell Ella that she looks ill?

....

....

Leila looked at the new girl, Beth. She was sitting on a bench in the playground. She was reading a book and not looking at anyone. She hadn't spoken to anyone at morning break either.

Leila remembered when she was the new girl and was too shy to talk to anyone. She sat down on the other end of the bench, took her book out of her bag and began to look at it. Soon, Beth looked over. Leila smiled at her.

b) Why is Beth reading a book?

....

....

c) Why doesn't Leila just go and talk to Beth?

....

....

DIG DEEPER FOR CLUES

① **You can find lots of important details by looking for hidden clues. This will help to build up a detailed picture in your mind.**

The wind was biting cold and the woolly hat and gloves did little to keep Matilda warm. She walked on, leaving icy footprints on the ground beneath her.

Q: What time of year do you think it is? Give **two** reasons for your answer.

Good answer: *It is winter. I think this **because** Matilda is wearing a hat and gloves and she is leaving icy footprints on the ground, so she might be walking through snow.*

② **How do you dig deeper for hidden clues?**

- You need to **look below the surface** of the text. This means finding details that are **not given** but *suggested* by the words used.

- You may find clues about the weather, time of day or time of year by **looking at the information more closely**.

- Does the text mention types of clothes, lighting or activities that could **help you to identify** the weather, time of day or time of year?

Digging deeper is like looking for treasure – you have to dig to find the gold!

NOW YOU TRY!

It had been a fantastic day. The sun was low in the sky and the children were exhausted, but happy.

What time of day do you think it is? Give **two** reasons for your answer.

....

....

....

....

HINT!

Make sure you use the word 'because'.

CONNECT THE CLUES

❶ There may be lots of clues in one part of the text, or they may be spread out across a few pages. Sometimes you have to put all the clues together to build the bigger picture.

The streets were bustling with people who walked with their heads down and umbrellas up, like ants marching. The bells of the church clock tower rang out across the city and, after the sixth and final chime, fell silent again. On the main road, car lights reflected in the puddles as the traffic zoomed along.

Q: What is the weather like? Give **two** pieces of evidence from the text.

Good answer: *It is probably raining because people have umbrellas up and there are puddles on the road.*

❷ How can you connect the clues?

- **Find the key word** in the question, e.g. *weather*.

- **Read the text** all the way through, then **highlight** the parts that are **linked to the key word**. This could be how people behave or descriptions of what is happening.

- **Connect the clues together.** E.g. people are walking with umbrellas up + puddles on the road = it is raining.

- **Be careful!** Some parts of the text won't be linked to the question!

TOP TIP ⭐

Connecting the clues is like a 'join the dots' puzzle. Link them all together to get the full picture!

NOW YOU TRY!

Read the example text again. What time of day do you think it is? Give **two** pieces of evidence from the text.

....

....

....

....

HINT!

The cars and the church are important here. Ask the question 'Why?'

Why were the car lights on?

Why was the church clock bell chiming?

QUICK QUIZ: MAKING INFERENCES

1 Read the text and answer the questions which follow.

It was a sunny day. Lots of happy, smartly dressed people were gathering inside the church. There was a photographer, and a woman who was making last-minute changes to the flower arrangements. Just inside the door, Stephen was talking to his dad.

'She'll be here soon – brides are always late!' said his dad reassuringly.

Stephen cleared his throat and fiddled with the flower in his jacket. He tried to smile, but he kept looking anxiously towards the church path. Inside the church, his brother Jack was talking to the vicar. Stephen wondered if Jack was worried too.

a) What is the special event?

    ....

b) What clues make you think this? Give **two** pieces of evidence from the text.

    ....

    ....

    ....

    ....

    ....

    ....

c) How do you know Stephen is worried? Tick **one**.

He is talking to his dad. ☐

He clears his throat and fidgets. ☐

He is smiling. ☐

He is thinking about Jack. ☐

2 Read the text and answer the questions which follow.

The little boat bobbed gently on the water. There didn't seem to be anyone in it. Michael approached the boat slowly in his larger ship. There was something strange about the boat that made Michael feel uneasy. He peered over the edge and studied the boat carefully. Through the cabin window, he could see enough packets of food to last several weeks. They were lined up neatly on a shelf and there were lots of bottles of water next to them, some unopened.

'Hello?' he called out nervously. 'Is there anyone there?'

The microphone for the radio was hanging down, and he could hear it hissing. Then he saw a man lying on the floor. Michael gasped. 'What had happened?' he wondered.

a) What do the packets of food and bottles of water tell us?

....

b) Why does Michael approach slowly in his ship?

....

c) How does Michael feel when he spots the man on the floor?

....

d) What can we infer (understand) from the text? Tick **two**.

It's a sunny day. ☐

The man on the boat is organised. ☐

The sea is quite calm. ☐

Michael really likes sailing. ☐

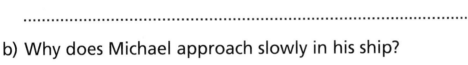

Wow, you're making great progress!

→ MAKING INFERENCES →

FINISH

DRAW CONCLUSIONS

① **You can use facts from a text to draw a conclusion, even though something has not been clearly stated.**

Sophia looked at the coat rack in the hall. Her mum's jacket wasn't there. The house was quieter than usual too. The dogs hadn't barked when she came in.

Look at the **paragraph** beginning ***Sophia looked at the coat rack in the hall***.

Q: What conclusion might Sophia draw from this?

Good answer: *Sophia might think her mum is walking the dogs because they didn't bark when she came in and her mum's jacket isn't there either.*

② **How can you draw conclusions from facts?**

- **Look at all the facts.** What do they tell you?

- **Check.** Does your judgement make sense? Is there any information that goes against your ideas?

    Sophia's mum's coat has gone = she must have gone out. The dogs didn't bark = they are out too. You don't have any other information, so a **sensible conclusion** would be that Sophia's mum is walking the dogs.

> Drawing a conclusion means putting the pieces together to make a judgement! It's got nothing to do with drawing!

TOP TIP ⭐

The **facts** are there to lead you to **a conclusion**. Follow the fact trail and draw your own conclusion!

NOW YOU TRY!

Arlo looked in the shopping bag to find out what he was having for tea. In the bag was chicken, pasta, tomatoes and the breakfast cereal he had asked his dad to buy. There weren't any potatoes or rice.

Look at the paragraph beginning ***Arlo looked in the shopping bag ....***

What conclusion might Arlo draw from this?

....

....

....

....

❸ Did you see? You know that Arlo is wondering what's for tea and that he's looking in the bag to find out. What does he discover? *There are no potatoes or rice* → *He would not have breakfast cereal for tea* → *The other things in the bag must be for his tea.*

PRACTISE AGAIN!

It had been raining for several hours. The river outside had already risen by 1 cm. Natalia was worried. The sky was full of dark clouds and the forecast was bad.

a) Look at the final sentence beginning **The sky was** ....

What conclusion might Natalia draw from this?

....

....

....

....

Jago looked at the map. He was still five miles away from the meeting point where he was supposed to be meeting the others at sunset. It was already starting to get dark, and he was tired and hungry.

b) What conclusion might Jago draw from this?

....

....

....

....

FIND EVIDENCE

1 **Sometimes you will be asked to find evidence in a text to back up a statement.**

> Evidence is the information that **shows** something.

Arthur couldn't get to sleep. His party was the next day. He was going to go swimming with his friends.

Arthur was excited.

Q: Give **one** piece of evidence from the text which shows this.

Good answer: *He couldn't get to sleep.*

2 **How can you find evidence to support a statement?**

- **Find the correct part of the text.** You might have to scan to find the part you need. Here you would be searching for information about Arthur.

- **Find the key word** in the statement = *excited*.

- **Look for evidence** that supports the statement. What is the **evidence** that Arthur is excited?

- **Use your own knowledge to help you.** If you had a party the next day and were feeling excited, what would happen?

TOP TIP ⭐

Always check that your answer is linked to the question. Does it back up the statement?

NOW YOU TRY!

Jannah went to the gym every day after school. She was working hard on her running and cycling. The school cross-country race was coming up soon.

Jannah was determined to do well in the race.

Give **one** piece of evidence from the text which shows this.

....

....

....

....

❸ **Did you see?** You need to **look for information that supports the statement. What would help Jannah do well in the race? How do we know she's determined?**

PRACTISE AGAIN!

We sat in a café by the harbour with a view of the sea. Some people had left their cars parked on the beach. The tide was coming in.

a) It was a bad idea to leave cars on the beach.

Give **one** piece of evidence from the text which shows this.

....

....

....

....

David's dog didn't like the postman. The postman came at the same time every day, and as soon as he put the letters through the door, the dog barked loudly.

b) David knows what time his dog will bark.

Explain this using evidence from the text.

....

....

....

....

USE EVIDENCE

❶ Some questions need longer answers. You might have to answer the question and then explain it with evidence from the text.

Donna was worried about her friend. She wondered how she could help her and what she could do to make her feel better. She'd promised that she would help her if things got tricky, and now was the time to prove it.

Q: What does this **paragraph** tell you about Donna's character?

Explain **two** features of her character, using evidence from the text to support your answer.

Good answer (features = **blue** text; evidence = **green** text):
Donna is a caring person and is also loyal. You can tell she's caring because she's worried about her friend and wants to help her. We know that she's loyal because she wants to keep her promise.

> **TOP TIP** ⭐
>
> Character **features** are the things about someone that make them special.

❷ How can you use evidence to explain your answer?

- **Look for information** that links to the question.

  - You are looking for **two features** of Donna's character. The first two sentences show that she is caring. **Evidence** = she's worried about her friend and wants to help her.

  - The last sentence shows that she is loyal. **Evidence** = she wants to keep her promise.

- **Always check** that your **evidence** explains the point you have made.

> **TOP TIP** ⭐
>
> You can check your answers are correct by looking for evidence, even if you aren't asked to give it!

NOW YOU TRY!

As soon as the police arrested him, Stan started to tremble. Questions were fired at him, but instead of answering clearly, he stuttered and stammered. How had he got himself into this mess? This wasn't how it was supposed to be. He was Stan, the brave one, who could do anything.

What does Stan **do** that shows he is nervous?

Explain **two** ways, giving evidence from the text to support your answer.

....
....
....
....
....
....

Watch out for evidence that isn't linked to the statement. It's called a **red herring** – something that looks true but isn't!

PRACTISE AGAIN!

The Cape buffalo is one of the most aggressive animals in Africa and has been known to attack victims with no warning. It's extremely heavy and has a top speed of 40 mph!

How do you know that the Cape buffalo is dangerous?

Explain **two** ways, giving evidence from the text to support your answer.

....
....
....
....
....
....

QUICK QUIZ: CONCLUSIONS AND EVIDENCE

1 Read the text. Choose the best answer from the options below.

> *There were lots of people standing on the platform at the train station. Everyone seemed to be quite angry, and lots of people were using their phones. There wasn't a train at the platform, but there was a big queue in front of the information desk.*

Tick **one**.

The people don't like getting trains. ☐

The train is delayed. ☐

The information desk is closed. ☐

The people have arrived at the wrong time. ☐

2 Read the **extracts** on the left. Match them to the **conclusions** on the right.

1 It was a cold, wet night, but Sophie went out without her jacket.

A She was very tired the next day.

2 Helena stayed up late doing her homework.

B They arrived late.

3 The football team's bus broke down.

C She was very cold.

4 The children went on a school trip to the museum.

D They saw a lot of interesting things.

3 Read the text and then read the sentences. Tick the sentences which are supported by evidence in the text.

> *Josh looked out from the holiday cottage. All he could see was fields. There were some sheep and a couple of trees, but nothing else. No shops, no other houses. What were they all going to do for a fortnight?*

There's a lot of green space. ☐

There are some animals. ☐

It's nice weather. ☐

There's a river. ☐

They will be there for two weeks. ☐

He's on holiday with his family. ☐

4 Read the text.

> *My name's Joe. My dad likes making models. He makes aeroplanes and sometimes cars. It's a very quiet thing to do, but I think he likes that. He has a desk with lots of paint pots on it, and I'm not allowed to touch them. He likes showing me the models when he's made them, but he's never asked me to help!*

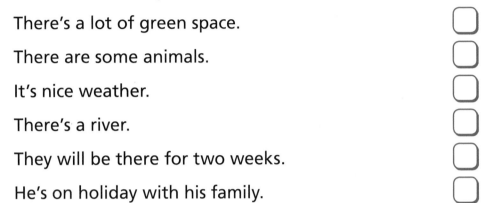

This **paragraph** tells you about Joe's father's character. Match the **statements** on the left to the **evidence** from the text on the right.

1 Joe's dad doesn't like a lot of noise.	A He likes showing me the models when he's made them.
2 Joe's dad is very organised.	B It's a very quiet thing to do, but I think he likes that.
3 Joe's dad is proud of his models.	C He's got a desk with lots of paint pots on it, and I'm not allowed to touch them.

Wow, you're making great progress!

→ CONCLUSIONS AND EVIDENCE →

FINISH

CHECK OUT MAKING PREDICTIONS!
MAKE A GOOD GUESS

❶ Can you say what might happen next **in a story? Making predictions** means using what you know about the story so far to guess the next part.

The children begged the king to believe them about the magic key. They told him about the room full of gold and how they'd fought the dragon.

'There's no such thing as a magic key!' the king replied, but then he looked at their faces and began to believe them. He wanted to see for himself if it was true.

Q: What might happen next? Include **two** things.

Good answer: *The king goes with the children and unlocks the door. He sees the room full of gold.*

❷ How do you predict what will happen next?

- **Read the story so far.** What are the **events** or **actions**?

- **Can you guess** the next likely steps?

- The children want the king to believe them → The king wants to see for himself so … you could guess that the king goes with the children, unlocks the door and sees the gold. Maybe he finds himself faced by a dragon!

TOP TIP ⭐

To help you predict the next part of a story, imagine you are writing it. What would you write next? There is no right or wrong answer as long as it follows on from what has already happened!

NOW YOU TRY!

Alice had been trapped for ages. She finally managed to pull open the window using her last bit of energy. She poked her head through the narrow opening and looked down. It was dark and smelly, but the ground looked soft. In the distance she could see a dim light. This was her only chance of finding a way out.

What might happen next? Include **two** things.

....

....

USE CLUES AND EVIDENCE

1 **Sometimes you have to use clues to infer what might happen next. You may have to give evidence from the text to support your prediction.**

Simon was nervous. It was the first time he had played in front of a crowd, but scoring goals was his special talent and something he loved to do. The ball was at his feet and all he had to do was focus and keep moving up the pitch. He was over the half-way line and heading towards the goal when a defender ran into his path. Simon paused and then darted around him. Suddenly he had a clear view of the goal. He took a deep breath and ...

Q: What might happen next? Give evidence from the text to support your prediction.

Good answer: *I think Simon will score a goal* **because** *Simon is a talented footballer and loves to score goals. He has moved around the defender blocking his path and has a clear view of the goal so all he has to do is kick the ball into the net.*

Be a story magpie and borrow ideas and events from other stories you have read!

2 **How do you make predictions using clues?**

- **Read** the content carefully and look for **clues** that might help you. What **important facts** do you know?

- Think **Why? What next? How** would you react? Use your own experiences to help you.

- **Link** to other stories you've read. This will help your ideas.

TOP TIP ★

Sometimes the title or the artwork can give you clues about what might happen. Remember to use all the clues to help you.

NOW YOU TRY!

Penny looked at the baby rabbit. It was sitting alone in the middle of the front path, looking scared. She decided to rescue it. As she carefully put one foot in front of the other, she could see the rabbit watching her and its whiskers began to twitch. The rabbit looked as if it might run away at any moment, but Penny moved forward very slowly. Suddenly, a large black bird squawked from a nearby tree!

What might happen next? Give evidence from the text to support your prediction.

....

....

QUICK QUIZ: MAKING PREDICTIONS

1 Read the text.

Jacob looked up at the tin of biscuits on the shelf. They looked so delicious. He'd finished his dinner, so he was sure that his mum wouldn't mind him having one. He had to pull up a chair to reach the shelf because it was a long way up. He stood on the chair and put one hand on the shelf. It wobbled a little bit under his weight.

a) Tick the ending you think is most likely. Tick **one**.

Jacob will reach the biscuits without any problems. ☐

Jacob will decide not to try to reach the biscuits. ☐

Jacob will try to get the biscuits but the shelf will break or he will fall. ☐

Jacob's mum will come in and give him a biscuit. ☐

b) **Find** and **copy one** word in the text which shows you that Jacob really wants the biscuits.

HINT!
It is an **adjective**.

....

2 Match the **beginnings** and **endings** of the story ideas.

1 A wizard loses his spell book.

2 A girl finds a mysterious house in the woods.

3 A sailor goes out to sea with an ancient map.

A He gets lost and faces lots of dangers before he gets home.

B There is a strange mirror inside it where she can see the future.

C He tries to remember what to do but keeps getting it wrong.

Wow, you're making great progress!

→ MAKING PREDICTIONS →

FINISH

CHECK OUT MAKING COMPARISONS!
FIND SIMILARITIES AND DIFFERENCES

❶ When we compare two characters, settings or themes, we say what is similar and what is different about them.

You may be asked to give an *opinion* and explain your answer!

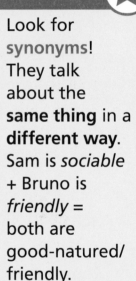

Sam – A large fluffy dog with big ears and huge feet. He's a quiet character who is sociable and enjoys cuddles.

Bruno – A miniature dog with a big personality. He's in charge of his humans but is friendly and loves going for walks.

Q: Write **one** way that the two dogs are similar and **one** way that they are different.

Good answer: *They are similar **because** they are both friendly. They are different **because** Sam is big and Bruno is small.*

❷ How do you make comparisons?

- **Find the important facts or events.**

- **Ask yourself some 'What' questions. E.g. What are the dogs like? What size are they? What do they like to do?**

- **Decide whether the answers to your questions are similar or different.**

TOP TIP ★

Look for **synonyms**! They talk about the **same thing** in a **different way**. Sam is *sociable* + Bruno is *friendly* = both are good-natured/ friendly.

NOW YOU TRY!

Beth wasn't as good at maths as Mia, but she worked harder and paid attention to the teacher in lessons. This meant that her work was better and she got good results. Mia, on the other hand, was chattier and didn't listen as well as Beth. She often missed important information, which meant that she didn't do her homework correctly.

Which girl will do better? Give **two** reasons.

.... *will do better because*

....

....

TOP TIP ★

Look for **comparatives** (e.g. bigger than ...) and **superlatives** (e.g. the biggest) when **making comparisons**.

FIND HIDDEN COMPARISONS

❶ **Sometimes the** similarities and differences **may be** inferred **or** hidden **in the words.**

The village of Ripton is set high up in the mountains among the forests. Few people live there and the harsh winter months make it a lonely, unwelcoming place. Instead, many people prefer to live in the larger village of Tunster, at the foot of the mountains. The weather here is milder and the farmers can graze their sheep on grass.

Q: Why would it be difficult for farmers to live in Ripton? Give **two** reasons.

Good answer: *It would be difficult **because** there are lots of trees rather than grass to graze the sheep. The weather is colder.*

❷ **How do you make** comparisons from inferred information?

* **Read** the content and **pick out** the facts or events.

* **What can you infer** about life for the farmers?

* **Fact** = the village is set among forests. **Inference** = there is less open space higher up in the mountains, so less grass for sheep.

* **Look** for comparatives, e.g. *milder*. What does this tell you about Ripton?

* Use your own knowledge to **check your answers**.

TOP TIP

You are given information for a reason. Ask: What does it tell me?

NOW YOU TRY!

Read the description below. Which village (Ripton or Tunster) would suit Freddie best? Give **two** reasons for your answer.

Freddie enjoys winter sports and loves snow, but isn't very sociable. When he isn't snowboarding, he likes spending time reading old books and relaxing in front of the fire.

....

....

QUICK QUIZ: MAKING COMPARISONS

1 Read the descriptions.

> Max likes cars and motorbikes. He plays football at the weekend and likes meeting his friends.

> Matt likes swimming. He goes to the pool every morning. He likes cooking and reading.

Now read the questions and tick the correct column for each one.

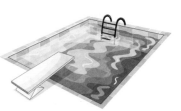

Which boy ...	Max	Matt
... likes being near water?		
... enjoys team sports?		
... enjoys spending time on his own?		
... wants to be with other people?		

2 Read the text.

> Our old house was cosy. It had a big garden and lots of space to play outside. It was very old, and things often didn't work. It was beautiful and peaceful in the summer, but there weren't any neighbours, and it felt lonely in winter.

> Our new house is more modern, and everything works properly. The garden isn't as big, but it's close to a playing field. We have some lovely neighbours and there's always someone to play with, which is the most important thing to me.

Read the sentences and tick the correct column for each piece of information.

	Old house	New house
Lots of space in the garden		
Things aren't broken		
Feels friendly		
Pretty and quiet		
Near a park		
Not as nice in winter		

Wow, you're making great progress!

FINISH

→ MAKING COMPARISONS →

ANSWERS

GET TO KNOW SATS QUESTIONS!

Multiple choice
... cold and scared. ✓

Ranking/ordering
Put a stamp on the envelope. **5**

Get a piece of paper and an envelope. **1**

Seal the envelope. **4**

Write your letter. **2**

Put the letter in the envelope. **3**

Matching and labelling
A hard-earned win ✓

Find and copy
a) Empty

b) The rain started to fall

Short response and open-ended response
Thomas ran away because he was scared of the spiders. We know this because he screams when he sees them.

PRACTISE YOUR READING SKILLS

Read questions carefully
a) Gloomy

b) It says that the trees stood 'spookily' and 'waiting to grab him', which might mean they are scary to the character.

Skim and scan 1
The second paragraph tells us what Sam thought at the end of the day.

Skim and scan 2
NOW YOU TRY!

Sunday

PRACTISE AGAIN!

a) The children took bags, jackets, coats and hats.

b) The children went to a new theme park.

Find information 1
Evie felt curious.

Find information 2
NOW YOU TRY!

The cat was sitting on the wall.

PRACTISE AGAIN!

a) The door was crooked.

b) 'Angrily' is the word that shows us that the cat didn't want to see Evie.

Use information
The phrase suggests the child is fragile/might break easily. / The phrase suggests that the child is very precious (e.g. to Marie).

Explain ideas
Maryam was excited.

CHECK OUT WORD MEANINGS!

Explain what words mean 1
It is empty.

Explain what words mean 2
improve ✓

Quick Quiz: Explain what words mean
1 a) careful ✓

   b) hard ✓

   c) The light was very <u>bright</u>.

Explain phrase meanings 1
Toby is thinking ... that he has missed the bus to school.

Explain phrase meanings 2
It was a nice/welcome sound.

Quick Quiz: Explain phrase meanings
1 a) rushed ✓

   b) getting in a muddle

2 1 C; 2 A; 3 B

3 became nervous ✓

4 a) ... done lots of things quickly. ✓

   b) take some time out

Explain how words affect meaning
pleasant, friendly

Explain how phrases affect meaning
Waves rose up like mountains

Quick Quiz: Explain how words and phrases affect meaning

1 The big dogs barked quietly in the garden.

2 Words about the train station/platforms: big, old, busy

   Words about what people were doing: talking noisily, running quickly

3 1 C; 2 A; 3 D; 4 B

4 a) quickly ✓

   b) When you turn out a light, it goes dark quickly. ✓

5 a) amazing ✓

   b) Because if something is out of this world it would be incredible or exceptional. Amazing is a similar word to this.

CHECK OUT INFORMATION!

Find facts 1

a) 1889

b) 324 m tall

Find facts 2

Elephants live longer in the wild. ✓

Find details 1

Vegetarian

Find details 2

Tim's mum was unhappy with the phone because it was broken/had stopped working.

Quick Quiz: Find facts; Find details

1

Maximum length	30 m
Maximum weight	150 tonnes or more
What do they eat	krill
Maximum speed	25 mph
Usual speed	5 mph

2 1 D; 2 A; 3 B; 4 C

3 a) Being an actress. ✓

   b) Ten years. ✓

   c) She's done more acting and studying. ✓

4 a) Michael hasn't always been a writer. He used to be a teacher.

   b) Some writers only produce a few books, but there are over 100 books by Michael Morpurgo!

   c) 'War Horse' is one of his best-known books.

Identify fact and opinion

NOW YOU TRY!

	Fact	Opinion
Warwick Castle is over 1,000 years old.	✓	
It is open to the public every day of the week.	✓	
It's interesting to learn about the history of England by visiting places like this.		✓

PRACTISE AGAIN!

	Fact	Opinion
The Junior Premier League has some of the best young football players from all over the country.	✓	
It's good for young players to have challenging games.		✓
They sometimes have to travel a long way for their games.	✓	

Identify true and false

NOW YOU TRY!

	True	False
Adele is only famous in the UK.		✓
She is from Wales.		✓
She has made a lot of money.	✓	

PRACTISE AGAIN!

	True	False
Colchester is an ancient place.	✓	
The Normans used the Roman castle.		✓
People only visit because of the history.		✓

Quick Quiz: Identify fact and opinion; Identify true and false

1 Tick: A; Underline: B, C

2 Parrot: A, F; Piranha: C, D; Rhino: E, B

3 a) False

   b) True

   c) True

   d) False

4 Two from: they have been on Earth for 400 million years; cartilage is softer than bone; some sharks are shy.

CHECK OUT SUMMARISING!

Order events

NOW YOU TRY!

Tom opened the door of the train. **4**

Tom couldn't move. **2**

Someone touched his shoulder. **5**

The train was moving. **1**

Tom started to panic. **3**

PRACTISE AGAIN!

Tom feels the SIM card in his pocket. **2**

The man asks Tom a question. **4**

Tom sees two men wearing masks. **3**

The man pulls Tom back. **1**

Summarise paragraphs

1 B; 2 C; 3 A

Summarise the whole text

NOW YOU TRY!

A lucky escape ✓

PRACTISE AGAIN!

An unusual find ✓

Quick Quiz: Order events; Summarising

1   The front door slams. **4**

    The phone rings. **1**

    Leah is worried. **3**

    Leah's brother is angry. **2**

    Leah's brother goes out on his bike. **5**

2   1. D; 2. C; 3. E; 4. B; 5. A

3   1 D; 2 B; 3 A; 4 C

4   a) An interesting palace ✓

    b) She didn't think she would like it, but she did. ✓

Find the message 1

You should not walk on the sea wall as there might be high tides which are dangerous.

Find the message 2

The message is to listen to advice.

Quick Quiz: Find the message

1   Don't spend all your money in one go. ✓

    It's nice to get presents, but it's better to give them. ✓

2

	For	Against
The skate park will be a good place for young people to meet.	✓	
There might be more things to find in the ground.		✓
Historians can find out about the Bronze Age from the objects found there.		✓
Skateboarding is a fun thing to do.	✓	

CHECK OUT INFERENCES!

Make inferences 1

sad ✓

Make inferences 2

Karen is excited. We know this because she's shouting loudly / bouncing around enthusiastically.

Look at all the clues

The character is nervous. We know this because (one from): his hands are shaking / he's sweating / he's pacing up and down / he could feel his heart in his throat.

Infer thoughts

Jack can't believe he's broken all the china. His wide eyes show shock and he shakes his head in disbelief.

Find hidden motives

NOW YOU TRY!

Toby wanted Marty to think that Dylan stole the bag.

PRACTISE AGAIN!

a) Lucy tells Ella that she looks ill because she wants to take her place on the team.

b) Beth is reading a book because she is new and she doesn't know anyone/is too shy to speak to the other children.

c) Leila doesn't go and talk to her because Beth is shy and Leila remembers that she also felt shy when she was new. Instead, Leila opens a book to show Beth they have something in common.

Dig deeper for clues

It is early evening. We know this because we are told that 'it had been a fantastic day' so it is nearly over. Also the sun is low in the sky so it is either early morning or early evening. All the information combined tells us it is early evening.

Connect the clues

It is 6pm. The church bells have struck six times, and it is getting dark because the cars have their lights on.

Quick Quiz: Making inferences

1. a) A wedding
   b) Two of the following: church; flowers; photographer; happy, smartly dressed people; the vicar; mention of 'brides'.
   c) He clears his throat and fidgets. ✔
2. a) Someone had planned to be on the boat for some time.
   b) Because he doesn't know what he will find and he's being careful.
   c) Michael is shocked.
   d) The man on the boat is organised. ✔
      The sea is quite calm. ✔

Draw conclusions

NOW YOU TRY!

That he is having chicken, pasta and tomatoes for tea. These are the items in the bag and he wouldn't be having breakfast cereal for tea.

PRACTISE AGAIN!

a) That the rain isn't going to stop. / The river will continue to rise because of the rain.
b) That he isn't going to get to the meeting point on time.

Find evidence

NOW YOU TRY!

One from: She went to the gym every day / She was working hard on her running.

PRACTISE AGAIN!

a) Because the tide is coming in.
b) Because the postman comes at the same time every day and this makes the dog bark.

Use evidence

NOW YOU TRY!

He is nervous because he trembles, which means that he starts to shake. He is also too nervous to talk properly, and stutters and stammers instead.

PRACTISE AGAIN!

The Cape buffalo is dangerous because it can attack people for no reason so you won't expect it. It is also dangerous because it is very fast and very heavy, which means it can cause a lot of damage.

Quick Quiz: Conclusions and evidence

1. The train is delayed. ✔
2. 1 C; 2 A; 3 B; 4 D
3. There's a lot of green space. ✔
   There are some animals. ✔
   They will be there for two weeks. ✔
4. 1 B; 2 C; 3 A

CHECK OUT MAKING PREDICTIONS!

Make a good guess

Alice might squeeze through the window and escape by following the light.

Use clues and evidence

The baby rabbit will run away. It already looks as if it might run away **because** it is scared and its whiskers are twitching. Penny is being very careful but the noise from the bird might scare it even more.

Quick Quiz: Making predictions

1. a) Jacob will try to get the biscuits but the shelf will break or he will fall. ✔
   b) Delicious
2. 1 C; 2 B; 3 A

CHECK OUT MAKING COMPARISONS!

Find similarities and differences

Beth will do better at school because she works hard and listens to the teacher.

Find hidden comparisons

Ripton would suit Freddie best because it is higher up and would have more snow for winter sports. He doesn't mind not seeing people and would be happy being indoors reading and relaxing in the harsh winter months.

Quick Quiz: Making comparisons

1

Which boy ...	Max	Matt
... likes being near water?		✓
... enjoys team sports?	✓	
... enjoys spending time on his own?		✓
... wants to be with other people?	✓	

2

	Old house	New house
Lots of space in the garden	✓	
Things aren't broken		✓
Feels friendly		✓
Pretty and quiet	✓	
Near a park		✓
Not as nice in winter	✓	

GLOSSARY

adjective a word used to describe something or somebody (e.g. red, interesting)

adverb a word that gives information about a verb, adjective or another adverb, sometimes formed by adding 'ly' to an adjective (e.g. slowly, anxiously)

comparative an adjective or adverb used to describe people or things and show differences between them (e.g. bigger than ...)

compound word a word made up of two independent words joined together

fact a thing that is known or proven to be true

metaphor a direct comparison saying something really is another thing

noun a word that is used for a thing, person, place, substance, feeling, etc. (e.g. table, thought, energy, London)

opinion a view or judgement about something

paragraph a part of a text that usually contains several sentences; each paragraph starts on a new line

past tense used to talk about things that have happened in the past, i.e. they have already happened

phrase a group of words that are grammatically connected

prefix a letter or a group of letters added to the beginning of a word or letters, which alters its meaning (e.g. **aero**plane, **il**legal)

simile the comparison of one thing to another using the word 'like' or 'as'

superlative an adjective or adverb that describes a person or thing as being more or higher quality than another (e.g. the biggest)

synonym a word that has the same or similar meaning as another word in the same language

verb a word that is used to talk about an action or a state (e.g. walk, happen, understand)

word class sometimes called 'parts of speech', the main word classes in English include nouns, verbs, adjectives and adverbs